HORSEM

MADE EASY:

How to Saddle Your Horse

Samantha Fletcher

To my husband,
and the love of my life
Jeff Fletcher

And thank you to my mother, Laura Barnes, for
giving me my passion for horses
And urging me to pursue it

To Our Readers:

Horsemanship Made Easy advises all readers to take notes (the key points at the end of each chapter) and bring these notes out to the arena with them. Index cards work great for this! Everyone forgets things when it's time to apply what you've read, so don't take the chance and bring the Key Points along with you!

Table of Contents

Case Study:
Lesson Barn Missteps

Apprenticeships are how many equestrians learn and progress through sports. I for one had many. It was while working an apprentice ship that I had seen, for the first time, a lesson barn that worked very differently from the way I had learned.

The apprenticeship was at a property that was next to a high end lesson and boarding barn. This neighboring barn had offered a higher priced lesson packages for students. These packages (even at the beginner level) offered students the opportunity to show up to their lesson with their horse haltered, tied, groomed and saddled. No cleaning, no bonding, no heavy lifting. The student would then be handed the horse, ride their lesson, then hand the horse back off to a handler and leave.

I have always been under the school of through that not only the pre ride routine is a HUGE part of bonding and learning about your horse, but also is a responsibility of the ride. The horse is working for use, so we must work for the horse. The additional addition of developing a routine to make sure the horse is tacked appropriately and the gear is in good riding condition is a major aspect as well.

The following edition of Horsemanship Made Easy will detail how to halter, groom, saddle and bridle your horse.

Before We Start

There are various terms that are commonly used in lessons and horseback riding (both English and western disciplines). If you are not familiar with any of these terms I strongly recommending purchasing my book, 155 Essential Terms for Every Equestrian (available on Amazon Kindle Ebook and Paperback, and Kindle Unlimited) in the Amazon store.

The Parts of the Saddle

Western

Near, or Left, side of a western saddle

Off, or right side of the western saddle

1. Pommel:
   Also called the swell. This is the front part of the saddle that the horse connects to.

2. Cantle:
   The back portion of the saddle seat

3. Skirt
   The leather shape of the saddle outline.

4. Gullet
   The underside of the pommel. This measurement is crucial in shoulder contact and movement on your horse.

5. Latigo

   The long strap on the near side (left side) of the saddle that attaches to the cinch/girth

6. Billets/off Billets

   The straps that connect to the cinches/girths

7. Front Cinch

   The front piece of tack that secures the saddle to the horse. This is held on by an off billet on the off side (right side) and a latigo on the near side (left side). A front cinch can be made of neoprene, wool, nylon, rope or other materials.

8. Back Cinch

   This is the cinch that connects the two back billets to the saddle. This should be fitted loosely and relaxed. The back cinch should also be hobbled (attached) to the front cinch to reduce the chance of movement and pinching.

9. Seat

   The portion of the saddle where the rider sits. Often made of leather, can be suede or polished leather.

10. Fenders

    The thick piece of leather that gaurds your legs. This also connects the stirrups to the saddle.

11. Stirrups

    The portion of the saddle that your foot rests in.

12. D-Rings

    Any metal ring that is in the shape of a "D" on the saddle. There can be many in any area of the saddle, used to affix straps, gear or riggings.

13. Rigging(s)

   The portion of the saddle that the off billets and latigo attaches to. Rigging can be attached directly to the tree or to the skirt of the saddle.

14. Seat Jockey

   The piece of leather or fabric that connects to the saddle beneath the fabric of the sear and shields the inside thigh from rubbing against where the fender and stirrup attach to the tree of the saddle.

English

1. Pommel
   The front of the saddle.

2. Cantle
   The back of the saddle, where the seat ends.

3. Seat

   Where the rider sits on the saddle, between the pommel and cantle.

4. Billets

   The straps beneath the flap that connects the girth to each side of the saddle.

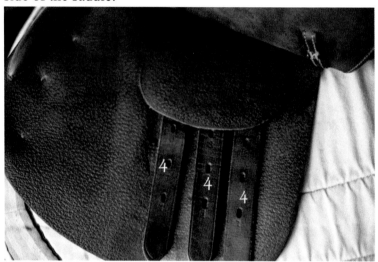

5. Leathers

   The strap that connects the irons to the saddle. Most often made of leather but not always.

6. Irons

   The metal or plastic piece of tack that connects to the leather, where the rider rests their foot while riding.

7. Knee Rolls

   The padded area of the saddle where the rider rests their knees while riding.

8. Flap

   The piece of material that covers the billets so the rider does not rub against these straps and buckles.

9. Skirt

    The piece of material that covers the buckles where the leathers connect to the saddle and that adjust stirrup length. This prevents some rubbing on the rider's leg.

10. Panel

    The cushion beneath the cantle and seat of the saddle that contacts the pad and the horse's back.

11. D-Rings

    Any piece of metal shaped like a D that is used to connect additional tack (such as a breast plate or martingale).

Brass D-Rings of an English saddle

The Types of Halters

Leather

Leather Halters are popular because of their functionality as well traditional style. These halters will give when a horse gets into trouble (stuck to a hoof or in a tree) and also are often able to be personalized with nameplates.

The negative with these types of halters are that the lean (the piece of rope attached to the halter that you use to direct the horse) is attached with a breakable clip. Though this will led the horse "break away" if trapped or panic, this will also send bits of metal flying when the horse does so.

Nylon

Nylon offers more easily with cleaning. You can brush they clean or wipe them off with soap and water It also offers cheaper price point than leather, and more options in color and even monograming.

Negatives of nylon halters include that they are much harder to break if the horse has to get out of trouble (the horse must rely on the metal clips breaking rather than supple leather giving way). Also, the same danger of the lead being attached with a thick snap clip that breaks off in pieces is seen with nylon halters.

Rope Halters

Rope halters are the strongest and safest option for the handler. The horse cannot break this type unless the rope is damaged or old. They can pull back and will be held fast to the tie point. This halter also offers added control as the knots tied on a rope halter are done in areas designed to add pressure to sensitive points if a horse acts up or pulls against it. This means the horse can be trained with this type of halter as they will not get away by acting up (so long as they are tied correctly on a well secured tie point).

The biggest negative to a rope halter is that it cannot be used for turnout. The other is that it will NOT break unless the rope is worn or damaged. This means if the horse slips, trips, is trapped or gets stuck in some way the halter will still hold. If the horse pulls back and breaks their tie point they will get lose and it will teach them they can act up to get away.

This will also be a bad situation if you tie the horse to something large and they dislodge it as it will be tied to them and "chase them" as they panic. Rope halters also require a specific way of attaching them to the horse so that the halter's knot can be load bearing and be easily untied. This requires learning a specific knot.

Other types

There are also shipping halters, breakaway halters and grooming halters. These are just as they sound and have different attributes for the type of use they were designed for.

Shipping halters are padded and easily able to break loose. This is so the halter does not rub the horse raw anywhere it attaches. It will also give way if the horse is in an emergency situation. These halters often are difficult to clean and annoying to attach and detach from the amount of patting around the horse's face.

A breakaway halter is often mad e mostly of nylon or cotton, and is similar to a nylon halter with one special addition: it has a buckle that is attached to the nylon/cotton with a short piece of leather. This offers added security in that the leather piece will break before the horse must break the buckles to get loose. Often this breakaway part is made from very cheap leather or artificial leather and will streatch or break quicker than a higher quality leather halter.

A grooming halter is specifically used for grooming the horse. It is meant to fit VERY loosely and leave enough room for the horse to be brushed, clipped or otherwise groomed without removing the halter. Because it is so loosely fit the horse must never be left without supervision as they could get loose or adjust it in a way that might scare or panic them.

Other Tack

Breast collar

The Breast Collar is the piece of tack that attaches to the front D-Ring on the off side of the saddle, wraps around the horse's chest and attaches to the near side D ring and lastly is clipped to the D-Ring of the Front Cinch.

The breast collar shown above is indicated by a black arrow.

Breast Collars are used to keep the saddle from slipping backward too much, or moving around. They are also useful when riding a horse in a tie down (a piece of equipment that goes under the bridle and around the horse's head). To keep a horse from getting a leg over the tie down strap it should be run underneath the breast collar then clipped to the front cinch D-Ring as well.

Wither Strap

A wither strap is used with a breast collar. This strap connects to the front D-Rings of the breast collar and over the horse's withers. The wither strap keeps the breast collar from interfering with the horse's shoulder movement.

Reins

Reins are used to move the horse's head, and are an aid in direction. This is the piece of tack that connects to the horse's bit and then is held in the rider's hands. Reins can be made out of various material (including: leather, cloth, rope or paracord) and come in a variety of types.

Haltering Your Horse

Before you're able to groom or saddle, the first step in every ride is haltering your horse. The method below is the correct way to tie a rope halter, detailed step by step. There are also leather, nylon or breakaway halters (among others).

First, you must put the long crown strap around your horse's right side of their head. Reach your arm across their neck and use your right hand to grab the crown strap, and use your left to grab the fixed loop on the near side of the halter.

Below the handler raises the crown strap over the horse's neck with her left hand.

Above, the handler scoops the horse's muzzle with the halter. Note: her left hand is grabbing the fixed loop on the near (left) side of the horse. Also, the lead is positioned below the horse's chin.

The next step is to threat the crown strap through the back of the fixed loop of the near side of the halter (as seen below).

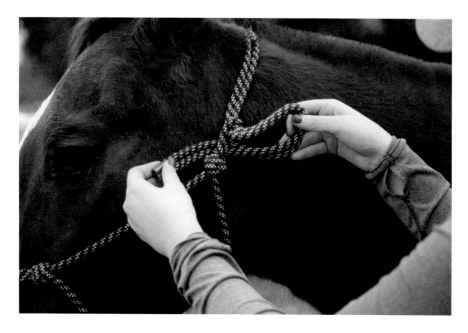

Above the handler wraps the crown strap behind the fixed loop.

Below, the next step in the know is to thread the tail of the strap through the circle that is made from the previous steps.

Below, a correctly tied rope halter. Two ways to check if you have done it correctly are: the tail of the halter strap should be pointing towards the horse's tail; and the knot you made would be around the fixed loop of the halter, not above it.

And here you see the finished know. This knot is a load bearing knot, which means it is easily untied even if a large amount of force is applied to it. This comes in handy if a horse spooks or pulls away from a tie point while tied. If the knot is tied improperly, you will need to cut the halter to get the horse free. A rope halter will not break unless it is damaged or worn.

Tying Your Horse

Cross Ties

Cross ties are most often seen in barns, or alleyways of barns. They offer a way to tie your horse to groom and saddle it without attaching them to a solidly mounted object. Horse's are very strong and can easily tear down a barn wall or door. Cross ties are mounted in a way that, should the horse panic, the cross tie itself will break away and the horse will be free. This is why cross ties should only be used with horse's who already are experienced with tying to a solid object without panicking.

A horse standing in cross ties.

To a Tie Point/Fence

When tying your horse to a solid object, you must first make sure that that object is indeed solid and secured before tying then proceed to tie a load bearing knot so that should the horse panic you can get the lead untied without having to cut the rope.

Your horse should only be tied with enough slack on the side leading to the halter that it can relax its neck naturally. Do not leave enough so your horse can graze or move around. This can lead to accidents or the horse getting its leg caught in the lead/halter.

While there are many types of knots commonly used in horsemanship, I find the easiest one to master is the Daisy Chain knot, and often begin here with my students. We will detail this knot in this chapter with step by step pictures.

Step one:
Loop the lead rope over the solid object.

Step Two:
Below, cross the rest of the rope over the end of the lead going to the horse's halter and make another loop. Pull this loop through the first loop.

Step Three:
Make another loop and bring it around the end of the lead going toward the horse's halter.

Step Four:
Bring the third loop through the second loop.

Step Five:
Pull the tail end completely through the last loop.

Horses are incredibly strong, and should one panic, they can easily tear off a fence, gate, door, or post that is not buried deep and cemented properly. If you're not sure, ask a more knowledgeable equestrian if a tie point is safe and anchored, or invest in a tie-point that will break away should the horse panic (such as cross ties).

Key Points:

- Tie only to solid objects that the horse cannot pull out of the ground.
- Horses are extremely strong animals and should only be tied solidly with load bearing knots to immovable objects.
- Tie the horse with only enough rope left on the side leading to the halter that it can relax its head naturally, no more.
- Daisy Chains are one of many load bearing knots used in horse handling.

Pre-Ride Grooming

After your horse is haltered and safely tied, the next step in saddling your horse is your pre-ride groom. This is an important step that should become routine every time you ride or saddle your horse. This give you a chance not only to bond with your horse, but to become familiar with your horse's body and check for any injuries your horse might have hiding in their coat or hooves. Heat, swelling, scabs or cuts should be checked before proceeding to your ride. Early detection is key in preventing accidents and injuries to both horse and rider.

Brushing

While this might seem tedious, especially if your horse appears clean, brushing your horse before and after a ride or workout is very important.

Be sure to make your way all around your horse's body and inspect any swelling, hear, bumps, cuts or scabs that might be beneath their coat.

First, start with a curry comb. This tool comes in various types, and depending on how dirt and how thick your horse's coat is at the time you can decide which to use.

A metal curry is better for winter coats and removing dried, caked on mud and gunk from your horse's coat. While a rubber curry will allow you to remove dried sweat and has the added benefit of spreading the natural oils of their skin into their coat, giving it a lustrous shine.

Above, the various types of curry combs.

To use a rubber curry, you should press fairly hard and brush in a circular motion. A metal curry acts more like a brush and should just be brushing in the direction of the hair growth.

Important:

Be sure to start at your horse's chest and work your way back and around. This lessons the chance of surprising a skittish horse.

Hoof Picking

When picking your horse's hooves you first must begin by standing to one side, near their front leg, facing their hind end. You will run your hand down the horse's leg to ask the horse to raise its leg up. Start with pressure on the back of the horse's canon bone, on the side of the tendon and increase pressure as your hand runs lower down the canon bone. Do not remove pressure from the horse's leg until the horse raises its leg for you to grab the hoof. When the horse lifts its leg up, cradle its hoof in the hand that is closest to the horse. Make sure you are supporting the hoof itself and not cradling higher up the leg as this will give you an unstable platform to pick the hoof.

A cleaned shod horse hoof

Be sure you position the hoof pick in your hand so that the hook is away from your face. This will allow you to pick the horse's foot in the direction away from you. That way you will not get pieces of whatever is in the horse's hoof in your eyes or face.

After you have finished with the front foot, you will move to the hind leg.

The hind leg is a bit different as the horse will put more weight on you as you pick these hooves and there is also a delicate joint called the hock that requires careful handling. You will ask the horse to lift its foot in the same way as the front leg. First you will run your hand down the back of the leg, applying pressure to the tendon at the back of the leg's canon bone. When the horse lift its leg you will need to bring the foot BACK, not out to the side of the horse. If you take the hoof out to the side you will apply pressure to the sensitive hock joint and can damage it. Bringing the hoof back will take pressure off of the joint. The easiest way to pick the hoof after you have taken it back behind the horse is to first support the horse's leg with your inside leg (the leg that is closest to the horse at that point). You will then cradle the hoof with your hand nearest the horse and pick the hoof away from your face, making sure to clear the hoof all the way down to the frog and along the horse's shoe. This will allow air to get down into the hoof and reduce the chance of infection or thrush.

Saddle Pad

The saddle pad should be positioned in a way that it covers and protects the horse's shoulders and also its back from the saddle itself. This is true for both English and Western saddle pads.

Remember you want enough pad that the horse's back is protected from rubbing, meaning the pad should cover at least just outside the saddle's shape. You cannot add pad to make a saddle fit better. This would be like wearing extra socks when your shoes are a size too small for your feet. The pressure points from a poorly fitting saddle will not disappear with more padding. You will need to first find a saddle that fits your horse, than use the correct pad for that saddle's shape. Keep an eye out for our book covering saddle fit in the new future. You can also visit local saddle shops or pay for a saddle fitter to come and take a look at your horse's back and give you recommendations.

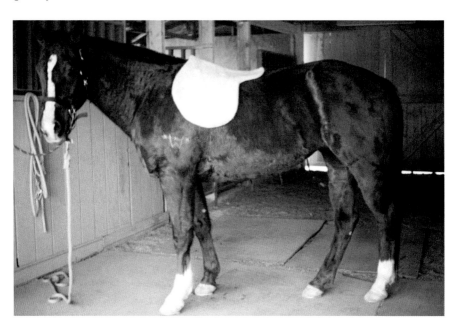

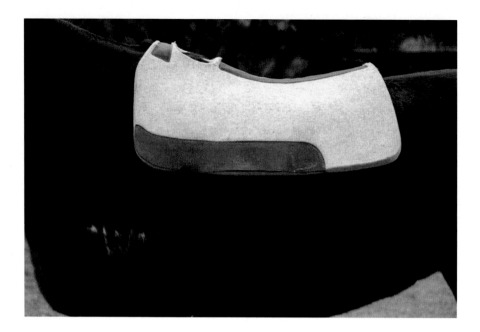

The first image is of an English pad and saddle in correct position. The second image is of a western pad positioned correctly on a horse's back. Be sure the pad covers the shoulders. The picture below is another type of English pad.

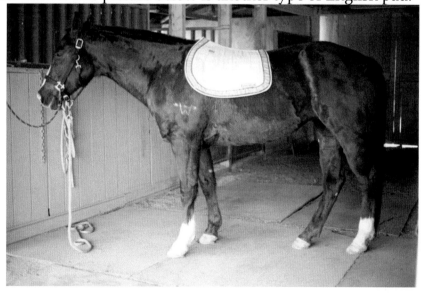

Saddling Western

Getting the Saddle On

After you have the saddle pad placed correctly the next step will be getting your saddle onto the horse's back. This is most easily done by "tossing" the saddle. To do this, you will stand by the left side of the horse, your left hand should be under the pommel, and your right hand should be on the back of the cantle or skirt. You will swing your saddle so that the fender and off-side (right side) stirrup swing over the horse's back. Be sure to gently set the weight of the saddle onto the horse's back and the pad. Adjust the pad and saddle until you are happy with the position.

Here a student tosses a saddle onto the horse's back with a swinging motion. Note the off side stirrup and cinches clear the horse's back.

Unhooking your Cinches and Breast Collar

Next, you will walk around the right side of the horse and unhook your cinch or cinches.

Unhook the cinches from their keeper and let them hand down, as seen below.

When the cinches are hanging, you should check to make sure the cinch is adjusted correctly on the off billet (the strap that connects the cinch to the right front rigging or D-Ring of the Saddle). The center D-ring of your front cinch should be positioned directly in between the horse's front legs. IF it meets the horse's chest off on the right side, adjust it down the appropriate amount of holes to get it centered. IF the d-ring hits off to the left side, adjust the cinch up higher on the off billet until it meets the horse's chest at the center.

The image above shows correct placement of the front cinch D-Rings, directly in the center of the horse's chest. If you cannot get the d-ring directly in the center, connect it so that the D-ring is just slightly off to the horse's right side. This way when the cinch is tightened fully it will pull the d-ring further to the left side.

Attaching your Latigo

There are two main ways used in western saddling to attach the latigo to the front cinch. We will go over both.

Both versions of tying the latigo start the same. You will first go down through the cinch, back up and down through the cinch again. You should only have to do this twice. More than twice and you will have too many layers to easily tighten the latigo.

First the student takes the latigo down through the front cinch

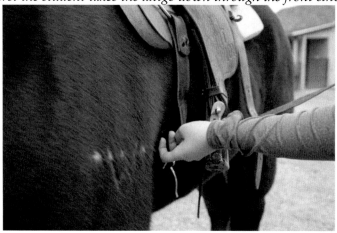

Next, she tightens the latigo just snugly, not tightly.

She goes back up to the saddle rigging (above), and then back though the front cinch ring (below)

Next, she pulls the slack out of both loops. Again, the latigo is not fully tightened here, just pulled snugly.

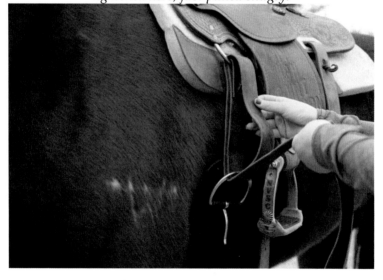

Now, we will discuss "the Texas T" Knot. This is used often and is very reliable (will not come undone) it is also easily tightened when in the saddle. Depending on the style of rigging the saddle has, it may, however, interfere with your left leg's position.

First, seen below, the rider takes the tail of the latigo back through the rigging, off to the left side.

Below, she pulls the slack out of the latigo.

Next, the rider takes the latigo around the front of the latigo loops, then back up on the right side of the rigging. From beneath the rigging ring, the latigo is fed up.

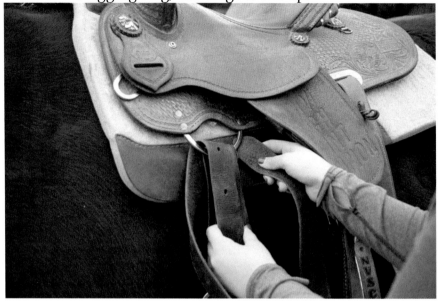

After the latigo is fed upward, it will then be fed back down through the loop created by bring it around and up on the right side of the rigging as seen below.

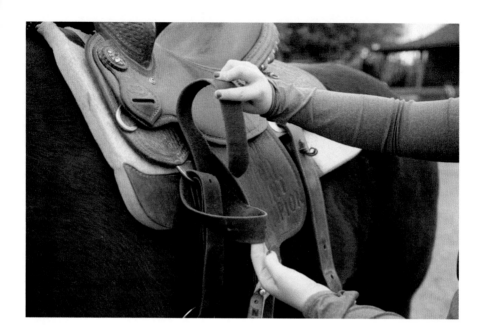

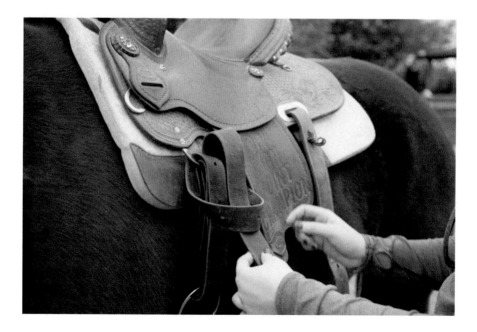

Saddling English

Some English saddles have pads attached to the saddle. If yours does not place the saddle pad on the horse in the correct position then simply lift the saddle onto the horse's back. Never ride your horse without some form of pad. Without a pad your saddle will rub your horse raw and lead to soreness and wounds.

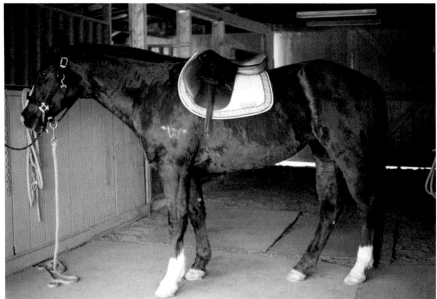

When the saddle is placed correctly you will connect the girth to the billets (the straps under the flaps of the saddle). English saddles will have three billets (this is in case one breaks or to aid in fitting thin or heavy horses).

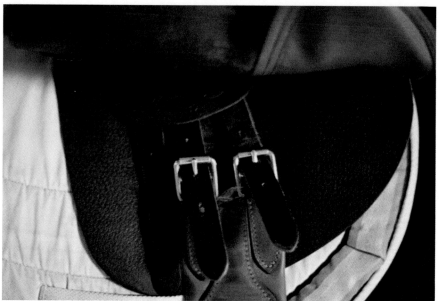

English saddle with Girth Connected to the Off Side (Right Side) Billets

Most often you will use the front two billets. If your girth has elastic on one side only the traditional way of saddling denotes having the elastic on the near (left) side of the horse. If you prefer to connect it on the off side it will not damage the tack or horse and is fine as well.

English saddle girth connected to near side billets

Connect the saddle snuggle and remember to check and tighten your girth before mounting.

English saddles have one additional step, you must let your stirrups down. Again this is most often done just before mounting and after tightening your girth so that the irons stay up and out of your way.

Lowering an Iron

Bridling Your Horse

Finally we will discuss bridling your horse.
To bridle you will stand on the near side of the horse. Reach your right hand above their head and between their ears.

Hand placement between the horse's ears at the top of their head

Grab the crown piece of the bridle with your right hand, as shown below.

Your left hand will open the horse's mouth so you don't hit or damage their teeth with the metal of the bit.

How to hold the bit when guiding it into the horse's mouth.

Use your left hand to touch the tongue, while your first two fingers will guide the bit between their front teeth. Be sure to press your thumb into their mouth at the corner of their mouth, this will guide your thumb into the gap between their incisors (front teeth) and their molars (back teeth).

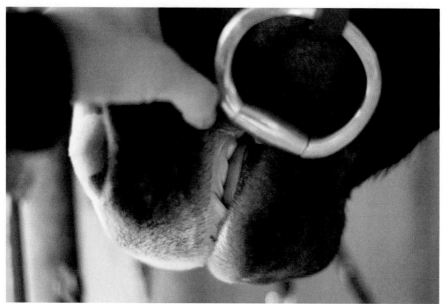

Showing the gap between the incisors and the molars, where you will reach to press the tongue to open the horse's mouth.

Use your right hand to pull the bridle up.

Point each ear forward then bring the bridle over your hand.

Put each ear forward and through the crown piece. Pointing the horse's ear forward before bringing the bridle back over the ears will lessen the chance of damage to the delicate bones that control ear movement.

Opening the horse's mouth to allow in the bit without damaging their teeth.

Important things to remember...

When unsaddling your horse, always reverse the order of saddling.

1. Take your bridle off.
2. Replace the halter securely on the horses head.
3. Remove the breast collar and hang it on the off side of the saddle.
4. Release the back cinch (if the saddle has one)
5. Release the front cinch.
6. Walk around the horse and secure or remove the cinches from the off side.
7. Secure the latigo on the near side of the saddle
8. Remove the saddle.
9. Remove the pad.
10. Brush your horse down (or rinse the sweat off if the weather permits)
11. Pick and check hooves (especially important if the horse has been out trail riding).
12. Return your horse to their stall, paddock or turnout and remove the halter from their head (never leave a halter on unsupervised).

Check your tack before and after each ride for wear and damage.

Spend time grooming your horse.

And (most importantly) enjoy your ride!

Recommendations

Thank you for reading! If you've enjoyed this Horsemanship Made Easy Edition check out our other titles at:

- *Horsemanship Made Easy: Lunging*

- *Horsemanship Made Easy: Transitions*

- *Horsemanship Made Easy: How to Buy a Horse the Right Way*

- *Horse-isms: 155 Essential Terms for Every Equestrian*

About the Author

Samantha Fletcher was born and raised in Arizona. After attending college at Arizona State University and working in the corporate world, she quickly decided that pursuing her love of horses was more rewarding than spread sheets, financial statements and managing employees of different motivation levels.

So, instead, she manages horses of different motivation levels and teaches riding near Peoria, Arizona. Samantha is a multi-award winner in various equine disciplines, including: Cowboy Mounted shooting, Gymkhana, Barrel Racing, Pole Bending, Equitation, English and Western, Trail, Basic Riding, Safety, Jumping, Ground Work and Horsemanship. She can be seen competing in events across Arizona and the South Western US with her mare, Bella.

Her book series "Horsemanship made Easy" can be found on Amazon in either E-book format or as a printed book.

Visit Samantha's Horseback Riding Instruction Website at *AZHorselessons.com* or at her book series Website *HorsemanshipMadeEasy.com*

Made in the
USA
Monee, IL